People of the Amazon Rain Forest

by Peggy Bresnick Kendler

PEARSON

Scott
Foresman

Editorial Offices: Glenview, Illinois • Parsippany, New Jersey • New York, New York
Sales Offices: Needham, Massachusetts • Duluth, Georgia • Glenview, Illinois
Coppell, Texas • Ontario, California • Mesa, Arizona

CONTENTS

CHAPTER 1
The Amazon Rain Forest and Its People   5

CHAPTER 2
History and Culture   9

CHAPTER 3
Life in the Amazon Rain Forest   13

CHAPTER 4
Modern Life for the Rain Forest's People   17

CHAPTER 5
The Future of the Rain Forest and Its People   20

NOW TRY THIS   22

GLOSSARY   24

Chapter 1

The Amazon Rain Forest and Its People

The Amazon River, located in the tropics in South America, is the second longest river in the world, running 4,000 miles from beginning to end. It is surrounded by the Amazon rain forest, the largest remaining tropical forest in the world.

The world's tropical rain forests are near the equator, between the Tropic of Cancer and Tropic of Capricorn. These rain forests have high temperatures all year, and they also see more than eighty inches of rain every year. Other tropical rain forests are found in parts of Africa, Southeast Asia, the South Pacific, and Australia.

The Amazon rain forest and river have more than 60,000 species of plants, 1,000 bird species, and more than 300 types of mammals. The rain forest and river also contain more than 2,000 types of freshwater fish and **aquatic** mammals, including such rare species as the pink freshwater dolphin and the giant otter.

Spanning an area of more than 1.2 billion acres, the Amazon rain forest covers about two-fifths of the entire continent of South America. It spreads across parts of nine South American countries: Brazil, Colombia, Peru, Venezuela, Ecuador, Bolivia, Guyana, Suriname, and French Guyana. The rain forest sits in a basin that was formed between 500 million and 200 million years ago.

There are currently about 200,000 **indigenous** people living in the Amazon rain forest. Indigenous people are those who are descended from the people who first lived in an area. The indigenous people of the Amazon rain forest live in small groups or tribes, and their lifestyles are probably very much like those of their ancestors.

Each tribe has its own way of life and its own customs. The tribes may get along with one another, or they might be enemies. People from one tribe may even speak a different language from a tribe that lives nearby.

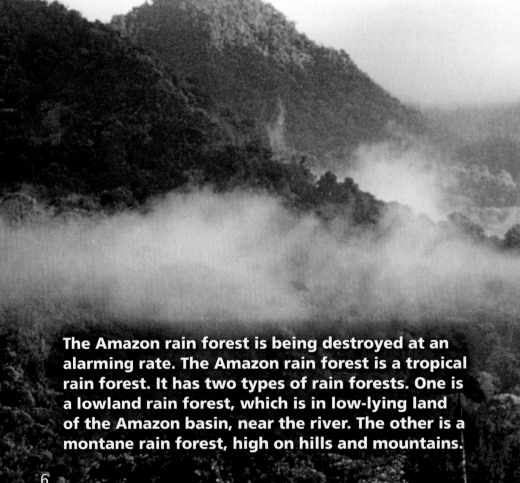

The Amazon rain forest is being destroyed at an alarming rate. The Amazon rain forest is a tropical rain forest. It has two types of rain forests. One is a lowland rain forest, which is in low-lying land of the Amazon basin, near the river. The other is a montane rain forest, high on hills and mountains.

There are two main types of tropical rain forests, which differ according to where they are located. Lowland rain forests are the most common types of rain forests. Most indigenous people, including those in the Amazon rain forest, live in lowland areas. **Montane** rain forests are found on hills and mountains, where it is cooler than in the lowland rain forest area. The montane rain forests can be enclosed in heavy mists, so they are also called cloud forests.

Far fewer people live in the montane rain forests of the Amazon than in the lowland areas. The people who have chosen to live high in the clouds have a very different lifestyle from those living in the lowlands. They are far from the Amazon River, and the plants that grow in this part of the rain forest are different from plants in the lowlands.

The Amazon rain forest is home to many different groups of people. Some have moved to the rain forest recently. Other residents include the *caboclos*, people who live in the rain forest who are descendants of indigenous people and European people. This group is sometimes called "the forgotten people" of the Amazon in Brazil because they have not been counted, but it's estimated that tens of thousands of caboclos live in the Amazon rain forest today. These people have lifestyles that are very similar to those of indigenous people.

Since the weather is so warm at all times of the year, the indigenous people of the Amazon rain forest wear very lightweight clothing, which is traditionally made of materials from the rain forest. Sometimes the clothes are decorated with dyes made from plants or vegetables that grow in the rain forest. Their clothing also might be adorned with feathers or other materials.

Chapter 2

History and Culture

Most scientists believe that the first people probably came to the Amazon rain forest from Asia nearly 6,000 years ago. These people may have come from Asia and traveled across North America before winding up in Central America and South America.

The very first people who came to the rain forest probably lived as hunter-gatherers, getting their food by hunting and gathering plants they found growing naturally in their environment.

Tribal Groups

Although the number of indigenous people in the Amazon rain forest is **dwindling**, there are still many who live there today. The indigenous people live in groups of as few as several hundred people or as many as several thousand people.

Most groups are very small and have fewer than 1,000 people. The groups of the Amazon speak at least 170 different languages and dialects.

The Yanomami are the largest indigenous group in South America. Yanomami still live in the same way that their ancestors did thousands of years ago; indeed, before the 1980s, the Yanomami had very little contact at all with the modern world.

The Yanomami live in the rain forest area of south
Venezuela and northern Brazil. There are four different
divisions of this group, and each has its own language.
Although most of the Yanomami are peaceful, some are
fierce warriors.

Another group of Amazon Indians is the Huaorani,
who live at the base of the Andes Mountains in Ecuador.
The group, made up of about 1,500 people, has always
needed to defend itself against other groups that
surround their land. Many of the group's members
are fierce warriors. They speak a language completely
unrelated to any other language.

The Huaorani are hunter-gatherers like most other
rain forest tribes. Some of them keep gardens, but they
also hunt animals for food. After a few years of living in
one place, they will move their homes to another part of
the rain forest.

The Kayapo of Peru are farmers. About 4,000 Kayapo
live in 14 villages in both the Amazon rain forest and a
nearby savanna. The Kayapo only became known to the
outside world in the late 1950s. They practice slash-and-
burn agriculture, which is a method of clearing land for
planting by chopping down some trees and then burning
them to add nutrients to
the soil.

The Awa-Guaja of
northeastern Brazil are
said to be that country's
last truly **nomadic** people.
Living in groups of five to
six people, the Awa make
temporary homes of palm
leaves. After a few years,
these nomads leave their
homes and find another
place to live in the rain
forest.

...usands of years, the lifestyle ...orest people changed very little. ...ges did come about, however, when ...e first Europeans arrived in South America in the fifteenth century and soon began to **exploit** the natural resources in the Amazon rain forest. They were not respectful of the indigenous people, their way of life, or their land.

In 1492, when Europeans first arrived in South America, there were millions of indigenous people living in the Amazon basin. Today, the number of indigenous people has dropped to just 200,000.

The early Europeans discovered many valuable natural resources in the rain forest, such as rubber trees that produced latex, timber from the huge trees, and oil. Some of the Europeans forced the native rain forest people into slavery. In time, many indigenous people died from poor treatment or diseases that the Europeans unwittingly brought with them, diseases for which the natives had no chance to develop immunity.

Chapter 3

Life in the Amazon Rain Forest

Although the peoples of the Amazon rain forest may speak different languages from one another and live in their environment in different ways, much about them is the same. For instance, since the weather in a tropical rain forest is very warm, the indigenous people often wear very few clothes. And for the most part, they live in closely knit groups and honor family life.

Tribal groups, such as the Bora and Huitoto who live in the Amazon rain forest of Peru, wear clothing made of bark cloth decorated with vegetable dyes. Bark cloth is made from the inside bark of a palm tree. Men and women in these groups adorn themselves with necklaces, feathers, and white or red body paint made from plants.

Members of these groups might sometimes adorn their bodies with jewelry, paint, and headdresses made of colorful feathers. When the men go off to fight other groups, they might paint their faces with inks made from vegetables. Some groups, use body paint and wear jewelry every day, while others adorn their bodies only during rituals or festivities.

All of the indigenous people of the Amazon rain forest have their own particular tribal customs. Groups such as the Piaroa of the Venezuelan Amazon dance and have celebrations for different occasions. They might wear masks that represent the spirits of animals, as well as costumes that completely cover their bodies.

The rich plant and animal life in the Amazon rain forest supports the lives of indigenous people in many ways. The trees and plants are used not only for clothing but also for shelter, food, medicine, and even transportation.

For instance, the indigenous people of the Amazon rain forest have always used the jungle's plants for medicines. Modern scientists have begun to use many of the rain forest plants to make new drugs to help people who have AIDS, cancer, and other illnesses. Many of them think that the rain forest is a potential source for many new drugs—including some "miracle" cures.

Brightly colored frogs are important creatures in both Amazon tribal rituals and hunting. A species of tree frog found only in the rain forest produces a substance called *sapo*. Sapo is used by some groups to increase strength before a big hunt. Another type of frog is used by the Yanomami and other groups when they hunt for animals. The poison dart frogs produce a poison that is used on arrows and darts that are blown through a straw-like device at wild animals.

Plants and trees have also traditionally been a source of materials for building homes and boats. Different groups have their own living situations, though.

The traditional Yanomami village is a huge house called a *shabono*, made of wood and thatch. It is built in a circular shape. Each family has its own living space inside the shabono. The Yanomami villages have between 40 and 300 people living in them.

Kayapo families live in separate homes, all arranged in a circle around a large open space. There is a men's house in the center and an oven at the other end as a gathering place for women.

Rain forest materials are also used by groups for transportation. To help them navigate streams and rivers, the Piaroa of Venezuela rely on the *bongo*, a canoe that has been dug out of the trunk of a tree.

Indigenous people also use the rain forest's wood to create works of art, carving wood into sculptures and using other materials such as palm leaves to weave baskets.

Farmers, loggers, miners, and the government all have built roads through the rain forest. Large oil companies have built roads so that trucks and equipment can get the oil out of the jungle. One road that was built through Yasuni National Park ran right through the territory of the Huaorani and other indigenous people. The road brought in loggers, farmers, and ranchers, who all began to have a bad effect on the rain forest. The damage that the roads, traffic, and outsiders are having on the rain forest is enormous.

Chapter 4
Modern Life for the Rain Forest's People

Even today, there may be some indigenous people living in the rain forest who have never seen anyone from the outside world. The jungle is deep, dense, and difficult to navigate. However, most indigenous people have had contact with people from the world outside the rain forest. Unfortunately, not all this contact has been good for the people of the rain forest.

The Amazon rain forest is being destroyed at an alarming rate. The destruction is having a devastating effect on the indigenous groups in the area who depend on the rain forest for their survival.

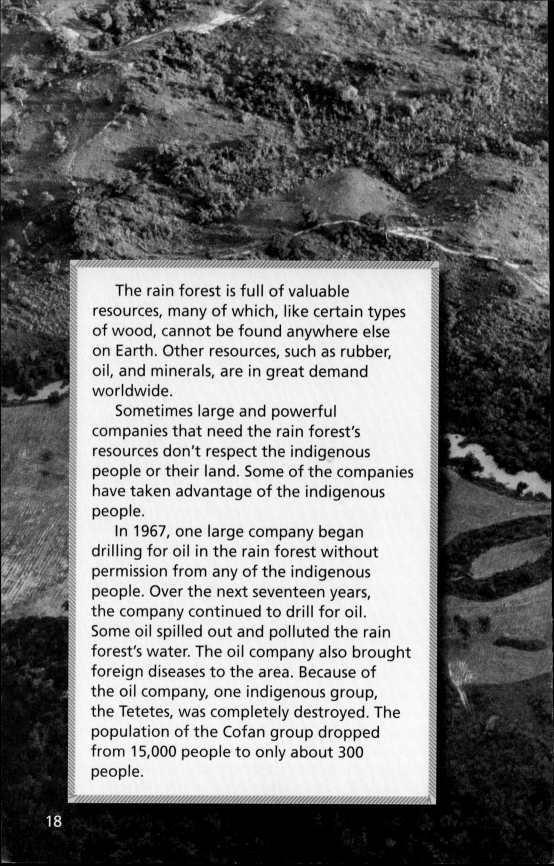

The rain forest is full of valuable resources, many of which, like certain types of wood, cannot be found anywhere else on Earth. Other resources, such as rubber, oil, and minerals, are in great demand worldwide.

Sometimes large and powerful companies that need the rain forest's resources don't respect the indigenous people or their land. Some of the companies have taken advantage of the indigenous people.

In 1967, one large company began drilling for oil in the rain forest without permission from any of the indigenous people. Over the next seventeen years, the company continued to drill for oil. Some oil spilled out and polluted the rain forest's water. The oil company also brought foreign diseases to the area. Because of the oil company, one indigenous group, the Tetetes, was completely destroyed. The population of the Cofan group dropped from 15,000 people to only about 300 people.

Deforestation

Today, outsiders are clearing the land of the rain forest for many purposes: to establish cattle ranches, to mine for valuable metals, to log, and to set up farms. Some of the areas of the rain forest are being burned to make charcoal. Many trees in the rain forest have been cut down for their valuable wood.

More than 20 percent of the Amazon rain forest has been destroyed, and more than 5 million acres of the Amazon rain forest in Brazil are destroyed each year. Each day, hundreds of acres of rain forest are being wiped out.

The effects of **deforestation** on the indigenous people of the Amazon rain forest are dramatic and devastating. There were probably millions of native people living in the Amazon rain forest about 500 years ago. Today, the population of indigenous people has dwindled to only about 200,000 people. Many groups have been entirely destroyed since 1900.

The indigenous groups of the Amazon rain forest may become extinct if the deforestation continues. Many groups, such as the Awa, have already been affected by the destruction of the rain forest. Their forests have been invaded by outside people, and some of the group members have been killed by the outsiders. The most alarming problem is that the forest that the Awa and other groups depend on for their survival is being destroyed by deforestation.

Chapter 5

The Future of the Rain Forest and Its People

The destruction of the Amazon rain forest is having grave consequences on the health of our planet. If the rain forest is destroyed, many species of plants, birds, mammals, and reptiles will become extinct. Experts estimate that more than one hundred species of plants and animals become extinct every day.

The rain forest trees and plants supply Earth with oxygen and remove carbon dioxide gas from the air. Some scientists believe that if the forest is destroyed, there will be too much carbon dioxide around our planet, leading to global warming. Then the temperature of Earth may rise and the polar ice cap may melt, causing the level of the oceans to rise. Coastal cities might be flooded one day in the future.

For the indigenous people of the rain forest, the future will present complicated problems. They must figure out how to preserve their very ancient and unique cultures even though their countries are very modern. Nearly every group living in the rain forest wants to hold on to its way of life, but they must do so in the face of ever-spreading "civilization" and the ever-increasing phenomenon of **ecotourism**.

Fortunately, the outside world has become aware of the destruction of the rain forest and its effect on indigenous people. Today, organizations around the world offer aid to the people of the Amazon rain forest, teaching them ways to face the challenges of working with the modern world. In this way, the groups are hoping to look toward a brighter future.

The indigenous people of the Amazon rain forest must live with the threat or reality of outsiders who want their natural resources. Some groups move deeper into the forest to escape the outsiders. Others have turned to ecotourism as a way to control their land, culture, and resources. For instance, ten groups have grouped together to form the Amazoncoop in Brazil. The cooperative runs a small lodge called "Tataquara" that invites visitors to see the rain forest and its people up close. Because the lodge is on property claimed by the groups and is run by them, the money visitors spend to stay in the lodge goes to supporting the tribes.

Now Try This

What Would Happen in Your Hometown?

In this book, you have learned that the Amazon rain forest is facing destruction by people who want to take away its natural resources or use the land in different ways. You have also learned how the indigenous people of the rain forest continue to suffer as their land is being destroyed. Their culture, their customs, their way of life, and their survival are being threatened.

Imagine that an outside company comes to your town and wants to build a new sports arena. They need permission from the town council to destroy most of your neighborhood to make room. The council is about to give its permission, because the arena will provide new jobs. But what about you? This business threatens to destroy your way of life by taking away your home and neighborhood, your school, the parks where you play, and the stores where you shop for food and clothing.

Think about the changes you and your family would see if the outside company destroyed your town and many other towns in your state. Then make a plan that will help your friends and neighbors save your community.

1. Write about your own culture and customs and what's important to your family. What would you miss most about your neighborhood if it were taken away from you? How would these changes affect your life? What would you do about going to school? Would you need to leave the area and move to another town? Would you have to move far away from family and friends?

2. Next, make a plan to save your community. How would you get your neighbors to help? How would you get your wishes heard by people in power? What would you say to prove that your neighborhood is more important than the sports arena? What different plan could you offer for providing jobs or for using another location for the arena?

3. When you have finished, compare notes with a classmate. Consider your classmate's plans and compare them to your own.

Glossary

aquatic *adj.* living in or growing on the water.

deforestation *n.* the removal of trees from an area that is mostly forest.

dwindling *v.* shrinking in size or number.

ecotourism *n.* tourism to exotic or threatened ecosystems to observe wildlife or observe nature.

exploit *v.* to use or manipulate to one's advantage.

indigenous *adj.* native to an area or occurring naturally.

montane *adj.* of or about a mountainous region.

nomadic *adj.* moving from place to place.